Inspiring Butterflies

A 27-Day Course of Self Discovery

Marge Richards and Ginny Zaboronek
Original artwork by Charlotte Garrett

4880 Lower Valley Road • Atglen, PA 19310

Copyright © 2012 by Ginny Zaboronek & Marge Richards

All text and images by authors unless otherwise noted in text

Library of Congress Control Number: 2011944042

All rights reserved. No part of this work may be reproduced or used in any form or by any means—graphic, electronic, or mechanical, including photocopying or information storage and retrieval systems—without written permission from the publisher.

The scanning, uploading and distribution of this book or any part thereof via the Internet or via any other means without the permission of the publisher is illegal and punishable by law. Please purchase only authorized editions and do not participate in or encourage the electronic piracy of copyrighted materials.

"Schiffer," "Schiffer Publishing Ltd. & Design," and the "Design of pen and inkwell" are registered trademarks of Schiffer Publishing Ltd.

Designed by John P. Cheek
Type set in Zapfino Forte LT Pro/Gill Sans Std

ISBN: 978-0-7643-3969-1
Printed in China

Schiffer Books are available at special discounts for bulk purchases for sales promotions or premiums. Special editions, including personalized covers, corporate imprints, and excerpts can be created in large quantities for special needs. For more information contact the publisher:

Published by Schiffer Publishing Ltd.
4880 Lower Valley Road
Atglen, PA 19310
Phone: (610) 593-1777; Fax: (610) 593-2002
E-mail: Info@schifferbooks.com

For the largest selection of fine reference books on this and related subjects, please visit our website at **www.schifferbooks.com**
We are always looking for people to write books on new and related subjects. If you have an idea for a book, please contact us at
proposals@schifferbooks.com

This book may be purchased from the publisher.
Include $5.00 for shipping.
Please try your bookstore first.
You may write for a free catalog.

In Europe, Schiffer books are distributed by
Bushwood Books
6 Marksbury Ave.
Kew Gardens
Surrey TW9 4JF England
Phone: 44 (0) 20 8392 8585; Fax: 44 (0) 20 8392 9876
E-mail: info@bushwoodbooks.co.uk
Website: www.bushwoodbooks.co.uk

Dedication

THIS WORK IS DEDICATED TO ALL THOSE WHO HAVE JOURNEYED WITH US ON THE PATH TO GREATER SELF AWARENESS.

Many Blessings
Acknowledgments

We are eternally grateful to Mark Richards and Roman Zaboronek for their unconditional love and support of our work. We are truly blessed to have them in our lives.

Contents

Introduction _____ 6
Day 1 Beginnings _____ 10
Day 2 Grounded _____ 14
Day 3 Survival _____ 18
Day 4 Trust _____ 22
Day 5 Self Esteem _____ 26
Day 6 Pleasure _____ 30
Day 7 Movement _____ 34
Day 8 Feelings _____ 38
Day 9 Strength _____ 42
Day 10 Confidence _____ 46
Day 11 Power _____ 50
Day 12 Love _____ 54
Day 13 Peace _____ 58
Day 14 Balance _____ 62
Day 15 Unity _____ 66

Day 16 Creativity _____ 70
Day 17 Self Expression _____ 74
Day 18 Truth _____ 78
Day 19 Communication _____ 82
Day 20 Intuition _____ 86
Day 21 Imagination _____ 90
Day 22 Visualization _____ 94
Day 23 Awareness _____ 98
Day 24 Wisdom _____ 102
Day 25 Spiritual _____ 106
Day 26 Knowingness _____ 110
Day 27 Inspiration _____ 114

About the Authors and Artist _____ 118
Butterfly Artist _____ 119
Butterfly Creators _____ 120

Introduction

The butterfly is universally recognized as a symbol of transformation. It also represents freedom, endless possibilities, and sometimes the personification of a person's soul.

A *27-Day Course of Self Discovery* has been created as a tool for insight, self development, and to connect with higher consciousness. Our recommendation is that you complete the *27 Days of Inspiration* book first and then use the cards and smaller guidebook to continue in a daily practice.

Working with these butterflies will facilitate well being in all aspects of life. Let your soul take flight as you step into the power and beauty that is within YOU.

Our lives are so busy with multi-tasking, that little time is left to nourish our souls. This book was created with the express purpose of giving you the gift of time for 27 days.

All that is needed is a commitment of 30 minutes each day. The optimal experience is for you to do the reading and exercises in the morning and carry out the assignments during the day. An alternative is to do the reading and exercises in the evening and carry out the assignment the following day. Carving out this small amount of time will yield immense rewards and put you on the path to a daily practice that can continue long after this book is completed.

The exercises are designed to provide you with a deep looking at your authentic self, while the assignments put it into practice. The inner journey will bring to light the best parts of YOU. There's a sacredness in remembering who you are at the core, and when this memory is integrated into your whole being you will discover a new way of being present with love and compassion.

The recommendation is that you engage in this book for 27 *consecutive* days. You will begin to notice subtle shifts along the way. Be assured that this is the movement you have been waiting for, the guidance that you have been seeking.

The progression of days moves you from a focus on your physical and emotional needs (days 1-11) to 4 full days of heart-centered experiences. Then, on Day 16, you begin shifting to the more metaphysical and spiritual aspects of self. Your journey ends on Day 27 with Inspiration.

The *Inspiring Butterflies'* Card Deck is based on the colors and aspects of the Chakra System, with each butterfly card depicting a particular Chakra.

The system originated in the ancient Vedic tradition and was incorporated into many Eastern philosophies. People in the West are now familiar with Chakras due to the popularity of bodywork and yoga. The word Chakra comes from the Sanskrit language meaning *wheel*. That is because the Chakra is depicted as a spinning wheel of concentrated energy located at different points in the body.

There are seven major Chakras and each one has a corresponding color, characteristic, and innate right. The well being of certain areas of the body are governed by a particular Chakra. It is believed that if all the Chakras are aligned and balanced, then the spiritual, mental, emotional, and physical well being of the person will also be balanced. Each Chakra is represented in our deck of 27 cards.

The Chakra System

Chakra 1 : The Base or Root Chakra

- Color is **RED**
- Ability to stand up for oneself
- Harmonious 1st Chakra = all physical needs are met
- Butterfly Cards: *Beginnings, Grounding, Survival, and Trust*

Chakra 2 : The Sacral Chakra

- Color is **ORANGE**
- The emotional self
- Social and sexual issues
- Harmonious 2nd Chakra = delight in the pleasures of life
- Butterfly Cards: *Feelings, Movement, Pleasure, and Self Esteem*

Chakra 3: The Solar Plexus

- Color is **YELLOW**
- Power and strength
- Self-control

- Harmonious 3rd Chakra = empowering ourselves and others
- Butterfly Cards: *Confidence, Power and Strength*

Chakra 4: The Heart

- Color is **GREEN**
- Balancing love of self with love of others
- Issues of peace, compassion and forgiveness
- Harmonious 4th Charka = give and receive love freely
- Butterfly Cards: *Balance, Love, Peace, and Unity*

Chakra 5: The Throat

- Color is **BLUE**
- Issues of communication and self expression
- Creativity
- Harmonious 5th Chakra = listen and speak in truth
- Butterfly Cards: *Communication, Creativity, Self Expression, and Truth*

Chakra 6: The Third Eye

- Color is **INDIGO**
- The right to see
- Vision, intuition and insight
- Harmonious 6th Chakra = trusting our intuition
- Butterfly Cards: *Imagination, Intuition and Visualization*

Chakra 7: The Crown

- Color **VIOLET**
- Higher consciousness
- Spirituality
- Harmonious 7th Chakra = heightened awareness
- Butterfly Cards: *Awareness, Inspiration, Knowingness, Spiritual, and Wisdom*

These 27 days will help you to remember that this one life is a gift and blessing to be appreciated and treasured.

Enjoy the flight!

Beginning the journey starts with being present in your body, feeling the life force within each breath.

Day 1
Beginnings

Upon rising in the morning, many of us feel a sense of new beginnings. We reflect on the day before; feel renewed at the possibility of second chances. Spirit gives us the opportunity to create a new beginning each day.

The sunrise behind this butterfly shows spiritual energy, or the life force, which transmits through all of us. The expansion of the butterfly's wings shows you that with each breath you are grounded in the present, yet hopeful of the future.

The deep earth tone in this butterfly symbolizes your birth into a new life. Your soul chooses several directions on its journey. Each direction presents an experience for growth. Trust that you are guided by Spirit through each experience.

This butterfly brings you the gift of life with new beginnings each day. Enjoy and create!

Exercises

As you start Day 1 of your journey, you are greeted with the *Beginnings Butterfly*. It reveals all the colors of a sunrise!

When you observe a sunrise, you are immediately drawn to the beauty of color. A feeling of peace and hope resonates throughout your body. This new day brings an opportunity for change. A new beginning! Create a visual picture of what you would like to see happen in this new day.

This is your day to shine. Pretend that you are already at the end of this day, and you're looking back with the biggest smile you have ever had. Why is that? What happened for you today?

Day 1 Assignment

As you move through your day, remember the vision of yourself from the morning; smiling and beaming at your good fortune. Simply by keeping that hopefulness alive, you are inviting the Universe to respond. The secret is to let it unfold, being present in each moment with no attachments to any particular outcome. Trust that you will be delighted and surprised with whatever comes your way.

I TRUST AND HAVE FAITH THAT EACH EXPERIENCE BRINGS SPIRITUAL GROWTH.

Whenever you awaken with a negative emotion or a feeling of gloom, open the page to the *Beginnings Butterfly*. It is your own personal dose of sunshine. Smile!

Living in the present moment gives you strength, stability, and a sense of personal peace.

Day 2
Grounded

In our communities today, many of us live apart from our families of origin. Sometimes this results in a disconnect from our roots, and our roots help to keep us grounded. Without grounding, it is difficult to feel safe and stable.

Red is associated with fire, and once the fire has finished burning, we are left with new earth. Earth is the element in nature that provides us with a sense of feeling grounded. This is the reason that many people feel peaceful at the beach. Just digging your feet into the sand makes you feel rooted and connected.

Orange and yellow continue the theme of "earthy," but at the same time this butterfly reminds you to notice the Source of the light behind all living objects.

This image tells you that to be grounded is to be in the here and now. All anxieties, fears, and self doubts live in the past or the future. Being in the now is where you find deep peace.

Exercises

As you read the list of words below, see if they apply to your own situation:

LACKING IN MONEY

DRIFTING

WORRIED

SPACEY

BORED

GREEDY

JEALOUS

UNROOTED

All of these words have to do with an imbalance in Earth, the element that keeps you grounded. Are you out of balance?

_____

When was the last time that your bare feet touched the Earth? How did it make you feel?

_____

Recall a time in your life when you felt the most *taken care of*. What was that like for you?

Day 2 Assignment

On your journey through life, it is important to recall and honor the people who brought you safety and stability. It may have been a parent, grandparent, older sibling, aunt, uncle, or neighbor. Locate a picture or memento of this special person and carry it with you today. For those who may not have had such a person, use a photo of a famous person whom you believe would have been a good caretaker or role model. Several times during the day, look at the photo and say the following affirmation:

*In this moment I rejoice within;
I choose harmony
now and always.*

Before going to bed tonight, reflect on the *Grounded Butterfly*. This image brings calmness, stability, and balance. Sweet dreams!

Survival

Being grounded in the knowledge that you have a right to be here brings support and hope.

Day 3

Survival

Moving through daily life, it is easy to forget to honor our existence and know that we have a right to be here. Many of us have felt less than others and perhaps not worthy of blessings and abundance.

The glorious reds and deep oranges of this butterfly connect you to the Earth and celebrate your birthright. You are then able to receive and participate in the gifts that are available.

This butterfly's background shows you that life can sometimes be difficult to navigate. You may encounter feelings of being disempowered, unappreciated, or disrespected. Know that this too shall pass.

The support and hope offered by this butterfly gives you a sense of comfort in knowing that you can overcome all obstacles in your path. It brings a message of hope: You can survive!

EXERCISES

Birth is a gift that many of us take for granted. We enter this world with much joy and love within our soul. We have expectations on how we wish to present these feelings to the world. Sometimes we find ourselves challenged by another's point of view, and we begin to not trust our truth and ourselves.

List 5 experiences since birth where you've felt 'less than' others. Include the emotion that was present in each situation:

_____
_____
_____
_____
_____
_____
_____
_____
_____
_____
_____
_____
_____
_____
_____

From each of these experiences a blessing was received. Write the five blessings and start each sentence with "I am grateful…"

_____
_____
_____
_____
_____
_____
_____
_____
_____
_____
_____
_____

DAY 3 ASSIGNMENT

Each blessing that was received enabled you to change something negative within your soul. As you go through your day today, anytime that feeling of being *less than* comes up, remember the blessings received. Say or write a statement of gratitude.

I AM ENTITLED TO SHARE IN ALL THE BLESSINGS OF LIFE.

Before going to bed tonight, reflect on the *Survival Butterfly*. This image reminds you that all difficulties and challenges will pass. You are a survivor!

Trust

Connecting to Mother Earth secures your place in the world.

Day 4
Trust

How can we not know that we are connected to every living being on this planet? Perhaps our culture, which fostered superiority based on gender, skin color, or physical stature, has created an environment of distrust rather than trust. Separation causes us to see the differences rather than the similarities; resulting in distrust of each other.

This image unifies earth and sky and shows that working in tandem creates the perfect balance. The deep maroon color in the wings represents the earth and keeps the butterfly grounded, able to find nourishment and support.

The sky blue shows you that this butterfly is able to alight and float gently above the earth, yet always trusting that she will return to her place of safety and regeneration.

The star like flowers anchored to the earth speak softly of their faith and trust that all is in Divine order.

EXERCISES

There used to be an old (very old) television show called *Who Do You Trust?* We're going to play that game today.

Fill in the boxes below with the name of someone you trust:

Selection	Who Do You Trust?
Family Member	
Friend	
Neighbor	
Co-Worker	
Boss	
Pet/Animal	
Community Leader	
Spiritual Advisor	
Author	
Politician	
Actor/Actress	

Now think about your answers. Which category was the easiest and which ones were a bit more challenging. List the two that were the hardest and the reason why.

Day 4 Assignment

Take the two that were the most difficult from the prior exercise and do a little research today. How can you make a more personal connection with someone (perhaps not the name you wrote down) in that category? Talk to a family member, do research online, ask a friend, or check a newspaper. Building trust happens when you feel a personal connection and shared values with someone. You will come to see that they are all here for the same reason, seeking acceptance and being honored. Expand your circle of trust today.

I AM A BELOVED CREATION DEEPLY CONNECTED TO SOURCE.

Take this sensation of trust to bed tonight. Set the intention to dream that you are the center of the Universe, connected to every living being.

Self Esteem

Accept and know that your strengths are valued and honored.

Day 5
Self Esteem

**M**any of us were taught at a young age that it was not polite to think too highly of oneself. While this has some value to live by, taken to extreme, this way of thinking does not serve us well.

This butterfly is a gentle reminder to speak kindly of yourself. By recognizing and valuing your own innate talents, it becomes easier for others to appreciate your gifts.

The blending of the golds and yellows serves as a light to guide your hidden potential to the surface. Once YOU are accepting of your unique gifts, the world will respond. Your own acceptance will serve as a mirror for others, allowing them to shine as well.

Let the deep red background be the platform on which you are seen as a person exploding with passion and love. Do not hold back now. Shout your message to the world!

EXERCISES

When was the last time you patted yourself on the back for a job well done? Today you're going to focus on YOU, and what YOU do, say, think, and feel that is good and positive.

There is no room for the negatives, the *what's wrong with me*, the way I'm *supposed* to be. It's all about who YOU truly are at the core of your soul. Let's bring it forward, applaud it, and celebrate the beauty of YOU!

Can you remember an incident from your past in which you felt really proud of what you said or did?

List at least 15 of your most positive attributes (you can do it!):

1.	6.	11.
2.	7.	12.
3.	8.	13.
4.	9.	14.
5.	10.	15.

Day 5 Assignment

As you go through your day today, ask several people to give you one positive word that they would use to describe you. Write each word down 10 times and say the following affirmation each time:

I GRACIOUSLY ACCEPT THE RECOGNITION OF MY STRENGTHS.

Before going to bed tonight, reflect on the *Self Esteem Butterfly*. This image brings recognition, feelings of self worth, and contentment as you drift off to sleep.

Pleasure

Lightheartedness enhances your ability to attract greater enjoyment into your life.

Day 6
Pleasure

This butterfly is fluttering by to remind you to have FUN. Much of life has become so serious, and we are constantly being reminded of what is wrong with the world. Simply by putting a lighthearted spin on your troubles, they will lift more easily.

Energetically, orange is the lightest of all colors. It is hard not to see the silly, funny, softer side of life when faced with an orange butterfly!

Bask in the glory of lemons and golds and be reminded of how the sun can make even the gloomiest day feel brighter. Let these colors bring out your playful side.

Try telling a joke, watching a sitcom, play with a child, eat ice cream, have a lollipop, tie a balloon to your mailbox, wear something outrageous, or call that friend who always makes you chuckle. You will be happy that you did!

EXERCISES

Say this aloud three times as fast as you can:

Suzy sells seashells by the seashore.

Children take delight in the simplest of pleasures and so will you today. This is going to be a lighthearted adventure as you will see the world through the eyes of a six year old today.

Let us start by reflecting back to your own childhood:

Selection	Favorites
Favorite Color	
Favorite Dessert	
Favorite TV Show	
Favorite Cartoon Character	
Favorite Comedy Movie	
Favorite Story	
Favorite Fairy Tale	
Favorite Vacation Spot	
Favorite Holiday	
Favorite Friend	
Favorite Day of the Week	
Favorite Month of the Year	
Favorite Birthday Celebration	

Now come into the more recent past, and write down the last trip that you took purely for pleasure. Where did you go, who were you with, what did you do that made it so much fun?

_____
_____
_____
_____
_____
_____
_____
_____
_____
_____
_____
_____
_____

Day 6 Assignment

Today you are to be conscious of laughter. See how many people you can make laugh today. Keep score and once an hour, look at the total and say the following affirmation:

My life is filled with joy and fun and laughter.

Before going to bed tonight, reflect on the *Pleasure Butterfly*. This image brings joy, laughter, and a smile to your dreams.

Connecting with your true inner talents and abilities moves you into the flow of life.

Day 7
Movement

What was your passion and what happened to it? Have you made decisions throughout your life that were influenced by others? Were they based on what you should have done and not what you would have loved to do? This butterfly is showing you that it is time to reconnect.

The orange in this butterfly brings to surface past passions and loves. It sets the stage for a lighthearted look inside yourself to uncover your hidden talents and abilities.

The background of this butterfly shows what can happen when you bring passions to light. A whirlwind of movement begins, and change happens.

Without movement, life becomes stagnant and heavy. With movement, life becomes an adventure with endless possibilities. Enjoy the ride!

Exercises

When you look at yourself in a mirror, you see the obvious, the physical. Wouldn't it be wonderful if you could see beyond the physical and see the beauty of your true self? See the many passions and talents that have been discarded or hidden over the years.

Imagine that you are holding such a magical mirror in your hands at this moment. How many hidden passions and talents do you see?

_____

_____

_____

_____

_____

_____

Select the one who is nearest and dearest to your heart and write down the reason that it was buried.

_____

_____

_____

_____

_____

_____

How would you feel if you were told that there was a very easy way to bring the talent/passion back to the surface? Read on.

DAY 7 ASSIGNMENT

Physical movement is the answer! Whether it is taking a walk in nature or dancing to your favorite songs, each movement that you make can release what has been hidden away. Today's assignment is to get into movement in order to bring your passions to life. No thinking, just get that body moving at every opportunity throughout your day. Take the steps, tap your foot, roll your shoulders, stretch your arms, breathe deeply. Each time, say the following affirmation:

I HONOR MY TALENTS AND MOVE INTO THE FLOW OF LIFE.

As you prepare for bed this evening, notice how your body feels after all that movement. Are muscles and ligaments that have long been dormant speaking to you? Just wait and see what else wants to flow through!

Honoring and validating your feelings invites emotional freedom.

DAY 8
Feelings

Much has been written about feelings and emotions. So many people have been taught to hide their feelings and told to "get over it" – a popular expression. This butterfly says to BE with it, FEEL it and OWN it. This is the secret to becoming emotionally free.

The salmon color in this butterfly image will get you in touch with your deepest emotions. Rather than burying your feelings, let them flow through words. Speak them aloud to self or write them in a journal.

The olive and cream background will support and encourage the outpouring of your true feelings. No judgment, just a space to be free.

Notice the shape of the image echoing in colors behind the main butterfly. By recognizing and honoring your feelings, you release them into the Universe and are free to be your true self.

Exercises

You are now beginning your second week of this journey. The first seven days have most likely connected you to lots of **stuff** that had been unexamined or not thought about for quite awhile, both positive and negative.

This is the day to let the emotions uncovered begin to flow.

Recall a situation where you had to bury your feelings. What repercussions did you experience in doing so?

_____
_____
_____
_____
_____
_____
_____
_____
_____
_____
_____
_____
_____
_____

Now recall a time where an experience with another brought you positive feelings about yourself. How did you feel emotionally?

_____
_____
_____
_____
_____
_____
_____
_____
_____
_____
_____

DAY 8 ASSIGNMENT

Today, you are to be in close touch with your feelings. Try to dig below the surface and really see the underlying emotion. For instance, you might feel angry, but when you look deeper, you discover that your anger is really due to feeling slighted. Take time throughout your day to examine these emotions.

I EXPRESS MY NEEDS AND FEELINGS AND LIVE AN AUTHENTIC LIFE.

The *Feelings Butterfly* will give you the insight needed to truly uncover the source of your feelings. Getting to the truth sets you free.

Strength within comes from a reconnection with self in a loving and accepting way.

Day 9
Strength

Loving and accepting yourself can be easier said than done, particularly when you have not lived up to your own expectations. We set the bar much higher for ourselves than we do for others.

This butterfly is here to show you that strength and beauty can be found side by side in even the most gentle of creatures. Notice the lacy, yellow wings that this butterfly has been given. While delicate and fragile in structure, the delightful yellow shines bright and strong.

The fiery orange and red background speaks of the summer sun. Hot and blazing on a mid-July afternoon, illuminating all. Are you ready to be in the spotlight?

If you have been feeling sorry for yourself, or perhaps hiding from the world and wondering why you are left behind, now is the time to step into the light and know that you are perfect just as you are.

EXERCISES

Did you know that there is only one of YOU in the whole wide world and that YOU are a unique blending of many different strengths? Today you will be uncovering and spotlighting your sources of strength.

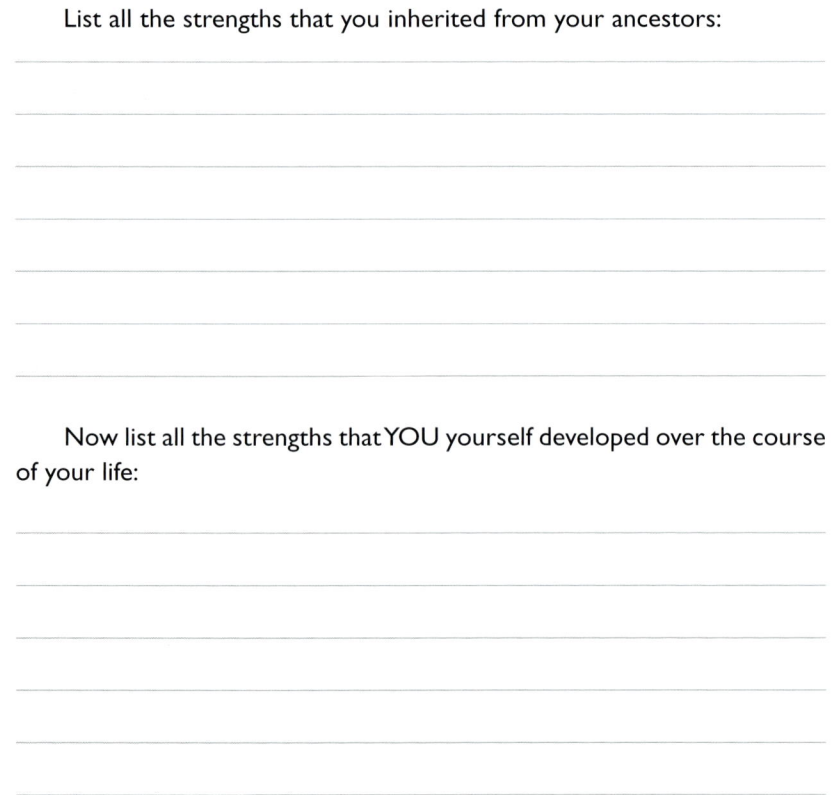

List all the strengths that you inherited from your ancestors:

_____
_____
_____
_____
_____
_____

Now list all the strengths that YOU yourself developed over the course of your life:

_____
_____
_____
_____
_____
_____

Now think about how these two sources have blended together to create YOU. Are you using these strengths to the best of your ability? Has it been awhile since some of these strengths have surfaced?

_____
_____
_____
_____
_____
_____
_____
_____
_____
_____

DAY 9 ASSIGNMENT

Today you are being asked to use two of your hidden strengths as often as you can. Be mindful of how you received the strength (inherited or developed) and gratefully acknowledge your gift. Say the affirmation whenever you recognize that you are using the strength:

MY SOURCE OF STRENGTH LIES IN FULLY ACCEPTING MYSELF.

Before going to bed tonight, reflect on the *Strength Butterfly*. This image brings acceptance in a loving way. Give a nod to your strengths as you nod off!

Respecting and listening to your inner voice gives you the power to act with faith and confidence.

Day 10
Confidence

When you are faced with a decision, there are usually many opinions and voices that you hear. It can be a bit overwhelming to decide which one you should follow. This butterfly is here to tell you that there is no better voice than your own. Just have the confidence to trust in yourself.

The mustard seed color reminds you that each time you really listen to your inner voice, it will grow louder and stronger. In time, you will feel a new sense of inner strength, that in turn translates into more positive action.

The various shades of green in this butterfly help you to remain open and ready for opportunities to come. Trusting in yourself and your Source will propel you to new heights and bring revelations and insights.

The bluebell flowers ring out your newfound confidence and tell the world that you are ready to fly.

EXERCISES

Let us begin by recalling a situation from the past (long ago or recent) in which you were full of confidence, poise, and assurance.

When did it happen, where did it take place, who was with you?

Now make a list of words that describe how you felt that day:

Now in your own words, write about why you felt so confident that day:

_____
_____
_____
_____
_____
_____
_____
_____
_____
_____
_____
_____

DAY 10 ASSIGNMENT

Imagine you have returned to that day of feeling so confident. Keep those feelings with you in as many situations as you can today, and notice what happens. Notice not only how you feel, but how others relate to you as well.

THE SOURCE OF MY CONFIDENCE ARRIVES THROUGH FAITH.

Before going to bed tonight, reflect on the *Confidence Butterfly*. This image will be a constant reminder to believe in yourself. Keep it by your bed, and in the morning say the affirmation.

Power

Self confidence and strength within yourself awakens your ability for personal power.

Day 11

Power

Personal power enables you to stand strong, think independently, and have emotional freedom. So how do you achieve personal power?

This green and white butterfly floats high above the clay colored background. This shows you that power is not connected to physical size or stature. A creature of any size can take a commanding presence.

Personal power appears when you are in alignment with your natural abilities. When you use these strengths in a positive and constructive way, then self confidence begins to flourish.

The final message of this butterfly is to remind you that you can tap into this power by believing in yourself. Your core being will be strong yet ready to float!

Exercises

Having power does not mean that you are operating from a place of ego. It simply means that you honor your gifts and talents and expect others to recognize them as well.

Sometimes we make others uncomfortable when exerting our power. This is especially true in a relationship where someone other than you has occupied the power position.

Can you recall a situation like this and were you able to turn it around? If so, how did you accomplish that?

_____
_____
_____
_____
_____
_____
_____
_____
_____
_____
_____
_____
_____
_____

Recall a relationship where you clearly held the power. How did that feel and were you recognized positively?

_____
_____
_____
_____
_____
_____
_____
_____
_____
_____
_____
_____

DAY 11 ASSIGNMENT

Did you know that there is a power position in every room? It's the place that is furthest from the door, but with a view of the door. Try taking that seat everywhere you go today; a meeting, the coffee shop, the train, at the dinner table, etc. Notice how your self confidence soars in these positions.

MY SELF CONFIDENCE PROPELS ME TO NEW HEIGHTS.

Before going to bed tonight, reflect on the *Power Butterfly* and your experiences in the power seat. Is this something you enjoyed or was it quite uncomfortable? Try it again tomorrow!

Remembering the desire to love and be loved will create a compassionate heart.

Day 12
Love

Most of us have experienced times in our lives when we have felt unloved or unworthy. When we are in the throes of that experience, it can be hard to remember that this is only temporary. This butterfly is here to remind you that love is always the answer.

For centuries, the emerald has been a symbol of undying love. The green in this butterfly is showing you that love is eternal, and serves as a gentle reminder that you are never alone.

Once you connect with the unending Source of love, you are able to see others in a new light. The traces of heavenly blue direct the heart upward to the Source. It is here that you will find the peace that will restore your soul.

The deep azure markings on the butterfly speak to the changing nature of life here on earth. The blending of the blues and greens tells you that love is just a blink away. It is yours for the taking.

Exercises

"We find rest in those we love, and we provide a resting place in ourselves for those who love us."

~Saint Bernard of Clairvaux

Quotations on Love:

"Love is a great beautifier."

~Louisa May Alcott

"Where there is love there is life."

~Gandhi

"The grand essentials of happiness are: something to do, something to love, and something to hope for."

~Allan Kay Chalmers

"The greatest science in the world; in heaven and on earth; is love."

~Mother Teresa

"You come to love not by finding the perfect person, but by seeing an imperfect person perfectly."

~Sam Keen

"May you live as long as you wish and love as long as you live."

~Robert Heinlein

"I love you not only for what you are, but for what I am when I am with you."

~Elizabeth Barrett Browning

"Love cures people, both the ones who give it and the ones who receive it."

~Dr. Karl Meninger

DAY 12 ASSIGNMENT

Select one of the quotes from the previous page (or one of your own on the subject of love) and write it down 10 times. Once an hour, repeat the quote 10 times. At the end of the day, you should have repeated the quote on love over 150 times! That's called spreading the love.

The more I accept and love myself, the more I can accept and love others.

Before going to bed tonight, reflect on the *Love Butterfly*. This image reminds you that love is always the answer. Set your intention tonight to dream of love. When you awaken in the morning, you will remember the feeling of being loved.

Peace

Acceptance and forgiveness allows peace to flourish within your soul.

Day 13
Peace

We all say we want peace in our lives, but what does that really mean and how do we get there? Peace is the absence of restlessness, heaviness, and anxiety, which are all symptoms of what happens when we hold a grudge or become too judgmental.

Notice how this butterfly floats on a background of deep ocean blue. This is a reminder that when you go with the flow you are more in alignment with the energy that the Universe is sending.

The pale green wings open the heart so that compassion and forgiveness can ignite your spirit. You are then willing to see others as unique expressions of their own special essence. You then allow others to simply be themselves, giving *you* the gift of peace.

The soft pink bodice is a gentle reminder to be delicate in your relationships and to love wholeheartedly and unconditionally. So when you find yourself tormented or obsessed with the behavior of others, join this butterfly as it floats calmly on a stream of peace.

Exercises

Have you ever tried to change someone else? It's almost always a losing proposition. The only thing you can change successfully is your perception of the situation.

Joseph Campbell writes,

"We cannot cure the world of sorrows, but we can choose to live in joy."

Write down your thoughts about his statement. How can you live more joyfully, more at peace, in the midst of challenges:

You can only give someone what you already hold in your own heart and soul. Looking at others with a peaceful heart allows that peace to be shared with them. What are some of the things you do to find peace?

_____
_____
_____
_____
_____
_____
_____
_____
_____
_____
_____
_____

Day 13 Assignment

Today, you are asked to remember the words of Thich Nhat Hanh: "If we are peaceful, if we are happy, we can smile and blossom like a flower, and everyone in our family, our entire society, will benefit from our peace."

My soul overflows with peace in my life.

Before bed tonight, look at the *Peace Butterfly* and think about how your acceptance of peace for yourself will change the world. This is a most powerful thought to hold. Peace be with you!

Unconditionally loving yourself and others brings a balance of joy and compassion.

Day 14
Balance

How easy it is for us to give! Whether we are a parent, spouse, friend, or co-worker, so many of us tend to put the needs of others above our own. Sometimes it is easier to forgive others while holding ourselves up to impossible standards.

This butterfly reminds you of the importance of balance in all relationships. The soothing green softens the heart and melts away any obstacles that may be blocking your ability to love yourself as you do others. Your heart must remain open to receive compassion and love.

The soft salmon and sandy beige work in tandem to help you see that the needs of each relationship will shift over time. It is important that you recognize when the focus should be on you and when it should shift to others.

The three images help you to keep in mind the dynamics between self, others, and Spirit. Honoring the Spirit present in all relationships keeps you in a higher consciousness that is brimming with love.

Exercises

Giving from your heart and not from obligation allows the Universe to bring joy to both the giver and the receiver. The vibration of positive giving represents unconditional love. If giving of your self becomes a chore, the Universe cannot return true rewards.

Recall a time when you felt good about giving? How was it received? How did you feel?

Now recall a time when you felt obligated to give? How was that received? How did you feel?

_____

_____

_____

_____

_____

_____

_____

It is important to recognize that the acts of giving and receiving will shift over time. A Mother unconditionally gives to her children expecting nothing in return, but once those children are adults, the giving and receiving should be reciprocal and more balanced.

DAY 14 ASSIGNMENT

Today's assignment has you looking at your closest relationships. Are your loved ones draining you or nourishing you? Are they listening to you or doing all the talking? Are they asking how you are or telling you about what they need? Are they speaking kindly to you or are they using a more demanding tone? Have they said they loved you today and have you said those words to them?

I AM BALANCED IN LOVE OF SELF AND LOVE OF OTHERS.

The *Balance Butterfly* will help you to see all relationships as they truly are. Be open for what is revealed.

Unity

Unifying love of self with love of others invites relationships to a place of compassion and harmony.

Day 15

Unity

Sometimes it is easier to give, give, give, without ever allowing yourself to receive. This situation can only bring disharmony and imbalance, and at its core is usually the feeling of unworthiness. Loving and caring for yourself must be in unity with your love of others in order for relationships to be thriving and healthy.

The predominance of soft, greenish-blue tones in this butterfly unifies the beauty of the sky and sea. Each a perfect complement to the other. No competing for attention, simply reflecting the peace and calm found in nature.

The presence of soft, buttery yellow represents the sun's rays that connect and touch both sky and sea. There is always a unifying element present in every balanced relationship.

The circles floating in the background remind you of how easy it is to be in harmonious relationships when both your self and others are given ample space to connect with Source.

EXERCISES

Today is set aside for noticing how much you give and how much you receive. Keep this book with you today, and as you move through conversations, activities and encounters, circle the *G* when you give, and the *R* when you receive.

FAMILY	SOCIAL	WORKPLACE
G R	G R	G R
G R	G R	G R
G R	G R	G R
G R	G R	G R
G R	G R	G R
G R	G R	G R
G R	G R	G R
G R	G R	G R
G R	G R	G R
G R	G R	G R
G R	G R	G R
G R	G R	G R
G R	G R	G R
G R	G R	G R
G R	G R	G R
G R	G R	G R
G R	G R	G R

Day 15 Assignment

As you circle the final *G* or *R* of the day, find some quiet place for reflection. Take a look at the balance or imbalance in your giving and receiving. Also take into consideration with whom and in which part of your life you are giving and receiving. Is it with your family, friends, or the workplace? What pattern has become visible? Record your answer in the space provided at left.

Say the following affirmation:

I AM GUIDED TO FORM HARMONIOUS RELATIONSHIPS AND TRUST THE SPIRIT WITHIN.

The *Unity Butterfly* will help you to harmonize your ability to give and receive in all aspects of your life. When you feel out of balance, simply go back to Unity and remember the message. Say the affirmation again.

Expressing yourself through creativity brings a heightened sense of acceptance.

Day 16
Creativity

Being creative can be the needed ingredient to spice up your life. Creativity comes in all different forms and can be found in work, play, and prayer. Follow this butterfly to find your own expression.

The blue flowers set the stage for a dazzling journey within to discover your source of creativity. What makes you laugh, what gives you pleasure, and what makes time stand still? Listen deeply to your intuition and do not edit what comes to you.

When you connect with your authentic source of joy, and express this to the world through creative projects, you will sparkle and shine.

Immersing yourself in whatever it is that makes your heart sing will result in a renewed enthusiasm for living life to its fullest. Give it a whirl!

EXERCISES

Let's do a little recalling.

When you were a child, what was your favorite rainy-day activity?

_____
_____
_____
_____
_____

When you were a child, what was your favorite sunny-day activity?

_____
_____
_____
_____
_____

How often do you do adult versions of those activities today?

_____

_____

Read the assignment on the right. Ready, set, go!

Old Word	New Word
Umbrella	
Butterfly	
Dolphin	
Sidewalk	
Dishwasher	
Bicycle	
Airplane	
Suitcase	
Spaghetti	
Lifeguard	
Snowman	

DAY 16 ASSIGNMENT

Today's assignment is designed to get your creative juices flowing. Invent a new word for each of the words on the list on the left. Be as wild and crazy as you can. You want to stimulate the part of your brain that may be out of practice.

Say the following affirmation:

MY THOUGHTS ARE ENRICHED BY THE CREATIVE SPIRIT WITHIN ME; I AM FILLED WITH RENEWED ENTHUSIASM.

Before going to bed tonight, reflect on the *Creativity Butterfly*. This image prompts you to find the child within. Fall asleep tonight by imagining yourself as a world famous_____.

Expression of yourself from a place of deep belief strengthens your right to speak.

Day 17
Self Expression

Do you find yourself saying words that don't ring true or saying what others expect you to say? Have you held back from speaking about injustices? Now is the time to practice self expression.

The blue in this butterfly brings you permission to delve deeply within and find the source and truth of your beliefs. Once connected to this truth, your words will become powerful and strong.

The two butterflies represent an interchange of honest communication between self and others. This continued dialogue reaffirms your right to speak and strengthens your spirit.

As you begin the practice of speaking from your heart, you will feel empowered within yourself and your relationships. Integrity and truthfulness are the keys to a meaningful exchange.

Exercises

While growing up you may not have been able to express yourself freely. Parents, teachers, and friends all had an influence on what you said. This may have created a block in expression that became habitual. Such a block can affect your creativity, your self esteem, and even contribute to severe shyness.

Let us take an inventory of how freely you were able to express yourself during your formative years with the following people. Rate them on a scale of 1-10 (10 being the freest expression):

People	Rating 1-10
Mother	
Father	
A Step-parent	
A Grandparent	
A Sibling	
A Teacher	
A Best Friend	
A Neighbor	

Now select the 2 with the lowest score and write below what you would have liked to say to them when you were that child:

_____
_____
_____
_____
_____
_____
_____
_____
_____

DAY 17 ASSIGNMENT

When you are not allowed to speak from your heart, you find other ways to express yourself. As you move through your day, be mindful of what happens when you are in a situation where you really can't say what you'd like to say. Keep a mental count of how often that happens and notice the emotion that arises.

I GIVE MYSELF PERMISSION TO EXPRESS MY TRUTHS.

The *Self Expression Butterfly* empowers you to bring all one-on-one relationships to a freer exchange of truth.

Speaking your truth liberates the flow of words allowing for honest communication.

Day 18
Truth

When we say things just because we know that is what others want to hear, we create a blockage in our ability to communicate honestly. This blockage can become habitual, and somewhere along the way, your authentic self begins to hide when not speaking your truth.

The heavenly blue in this butterfly shows you that your spirit will soar when you speak the truth. Rising above your fears of being judged for your words, you will be given new strength.

Just as the gold shadow is left behind, so too is your spirit when you hide the truth. Speaking from the heart will always set you free.

Begin by speaking the truth to yourself. An honest conversation can bring many things to light and begin to give you the courage to then speak your truth to others. Practice in a small way until your fears are subdued.

Exercises

Yesterday you went back to the past and recalled those to whom you could not speak freely.

Today you will focus on speaking with an open heart. You will experience how that has an impact on your emotional and physical well being. When the heart is open, your exchanges with others are smoother and easier. When your heart is closed due to blockages or fear, your words become constricted.

Let us demonstrate:

1. Sit in a comfortable position with your spine straight and head aligned with the energy above.
2. Close your eyes and spread your arms while visualizing your heart being open and receptive.
3. Now one by one, bring into your vision the people who are closest to you.
4. Hold their image for just a minute, and then think about how that felt in your body.

Did you smile, were you at ease in that vulnerable position, did you feel relaxed? Repeat with each person.

Now assume the same position but this time bring in those people with whom you experience difficulties when expressing yourself.

Repeat the same process bringing them in for a minute and then reflecting. How did that feel this time? Did you frown, did your eyes tense up, did your body tighten, did you feel vulnerable?

When you finish, open your eyes, take a deep breath, and say aloud:

"I AM NOW OPEN AND TRUTHFUL WITH YOU AND I SEND YOU BLESSINGS."

Day 18 Assignment

The freedom that you feel from speaking your truth to others is complete when you trust and have faith in who you are. Your body is able to give you clues if you pay attention. As you go through the day today, be aware of how your body reacts in the presence of truth, and what happens in the presence of false words. Think back to the physical sensations you felt earlier. Which ones are showing up? If the fearful, constricted ones are present you can transform them by using the saying from above, "*I am now open and truthful with you and I send you blessings.*"

My words are validated by the presence of truth.

Before going to bed tonight, reflect on the *Truth Butterfly*. This image gives you the confidence to believe in yourself and your truth. Each time you speak your truth, you will become stronger and less intimidated by others.

Believing in yourself enhances your ability to communicate with focus and clarity.

Day 19
Communication

Have you ever been in a group situation where you are called upon to speak, and no words come? The physical manifestations become tangled words, sweaty palms and no eye contact. Just the opposite is true if you are speaking from a position of confidence within yourself. When you believe in yourself, others will listen and resonate with your words.

These butterflies reflect the inner strength available to you when you speak from a deep-seated conviction. Blue represents water, and water will always help to keep you in the flow when communicating with others.

You can always see the stars more clearly against the deep blue of the evening sky. In this image, the blues and purples inspire you to find the right words to make your message crystal clear.

The next time you find yourself in a position to speak to others, remember these butterflies and believe in yourself. Your soul will feel radiant, mesmerizing and enchanting.

Exercises

For the last two days, your focus has been on speaking your truth; first as a child to adult, then as adult to adult. Now you're going to focus on speaking your truth in the context of a larger group. This could be in the family, the workplace, or the community.

Most often, when you hold back in a group, it's simply because you are unsure of yourself, afraid that people will judge or label you.

A wonderful place to start is with the physical space itself. Energy in a room can become overwhelming when many voices are present. So you are going to learn some simple ways to give you an advantage when preparing to speak in a group.

Begin by being the first to arrive. As you cross the threshold of the room, in your mind's eye, bring a beam of light behind you. Once in the room, visualize this light expanding and clearing the room of any old, stuck energy. Take a deep breath and feel the coolness of the cleared space.

As each person arrives, greet them silently with an open heart. Visualize the beam of light extending from your heart to theirs, and then the light is returned from their heart to yours. Connecting with others at this heart level opens the way for honest and meaningful dialogue.

Day 19 Assignment

If you do not have an opportunity to practice today in a group setting, try the heart connecting exercise one-on-one. At the end of the day write down your experiences with this heart work. Record your answer in the space provided at right.:

I COMMUNICATE FROM A PLACE OF INNER STRENGTH

Drift off to sleep tonight remembering the strength you showed today!

Intuition

Trusting your intuition creates an awakening of inner power.

Day 20

Intuition

For the last few hundred years, we have been taught that science has all the answers. We are rediscovering the power of listening to our intuition. This butterfly awakens your inner voice and helps you to listen through your sense of knowing.

The green background in this image brings to mind the freshness of Spring. As your intuition matures from the seedlings in Spring to the fullness of Summer, you will find that your own guidance will blossom from a position of strength and wisdom.

In Eastern cultures there is strength in the balance of Yin and Yang energies. The predominance of blue in this butterfly helps to keep an even flow between the powers of mind and Spirit, giving each realm their due.

Blue also brings to mind the depths of the ocean. Your intuition can be found by tapping deeply within yourself. Once brought to the surface, your ideas and thoughts are as crystal clear and refreshing as a well spring of water. Have trust!

Exercises

You may think that powers of intuition are reserved for psychics and mystics. The truth is that everyone has these abilities. The difference is that some people have more experiences than others because they have developed these gifts and welcome them.

Carl Jung called it *synchronicity*. An example would be if the phone rings, you pick it up, and it is someone you were just thinking about. Or your old roommate has been on your mind lately and then you take a vacation to New York, walk down the city street and there she is coming the other way.

Recall some of your own examples of synchronicity:

Oftentimes, your body will serve as a guide in developing intuition. You may feel a tingle at the back of the neck, a tightening in your stomach, or a flash of light. If your body was your guide, which part would it be and how would you react?

Day 20 Assignment

Today's assignment is to pay attention to your synchronistic events. Look for, and expect them to happen. You will be surprised how many times today you will find them, once you are aware.

I GAIN STRENGTH BY LISTENING TO MY THOUGHTS AND INNER GUIDANCE.

Before going to bed tonight, reflect on the *Intuition Butterfly*. This image awakens your intuitive powers and sets the stage for more to happen each day.

Imagination

Endless possibilities
are brought to life
through magic.

Day 21
Imagination

Have you ever listened to little children playing together? You will often hear them begin by saying, "Let us pretend….." Children also drift to sleep at night by using their imagination. When was the last time this happened to you? As we grow older, our more practical serious side is likely to dominate. This butterfly is here to set you free.

This butterfly's midnight blue color activates your deeper intuitive side and brings you to the place of your dreams. Here anything is possible. Be anyone you wish, from a princess to a president to an astronaut exploring the universe.

The tropical teal brings a dimension of lightness to the voice within. We tend to be serious with ourselves, and this color really works to remind you that life can be fun!

The dazzling violet background of swirls and curls supports you in taking a lighthearted look at life. You float along enjoying the magic that happens while allowing your imagination to fully expand in consciousness.

EXERCISES

Today is all about FUN! Your imagination is going to have free reign to be crazy, ridiculous, and exotic.

Fill in the blanks with whatever comes to mind. All of the sentences must be preceded by the word *"Imagine "*

If I was a spice, it would be:

If I was a color that could fill a room, it would be :

If I was wealthy the charity I support would be:

If I was in a Broadway Show, my character would be:

If I did not have to work anymore, I would spend my days:

If my hidden talent of _____ was discovered, I could:

If only my parents had encouraged me to:

If I could vacation anywhere in the world, I would go to:

If I could make one person in my life be well, it would be:

If I were an animal, I would be a:

If I went to heaven, it would look like:

If I was given a surprise party today, it would be at:

If I won the lottery, I would:

If I could change where I live, I would live in:

If I could bring peace to earth, I would:

DAY 21 ASSIGNMENT

Just imagine your assignment today.

I OVERFLOW WITH UNLIMITED POTENTIAL

Dream the impossible tonight. The *Imagination Butterfly* is with you.

Visualization

Feeling your meaningful thoughts brings your vision to life.

Day 22
Visualization

Long before we began to write the history of our people, images were used to convey important life events. Many of our 21st-century spiritual teachers have once again brought the practice of visualization to light as a tool for self actualization.

This butterfly adds the dimension of feeling to a vision. It is not enough to see your manifestation; you must feel it. The dark royal blue awakens your ability to see on a deeper level.

The amethyst color then sends this deeper vibration throughout your body pronouncing that all things are possible. You feel in every sense of the word that your dreams can come true.

What is your heart's desire? Create it, feel it, see it. Imagine, how will you feel in body, mind and spirit when it happens? Let the thrill of fulfillment resonate in every inch of your being!

EXERCISES

Practice makes perfect! Today you are going to be experiencing the emotions of joy, excitement, and fulfillment in your body.

The reflection for this butterfly talks about how just **seeing** your wishes come true is not enough. You have to **feel** them come true. Before anything can come into manifestation it must begin as a thought, conscious or unconscious. From there, the thought materializes into physical reality. You know how powerful your thoughts are, so now add on the impact of the physical body and you have a recipe for success.

Each scenario must be acted out as if it had really and truly happened to you. Shout it, move around, dance, laugh out loud. Do whatever you want, but you have to experience it as if it had already happened!

- You just won a $1,000,000!
- The producer just called and they want to make a movie about your life!
- You have won the vacation of your dreams!
- Your lost pet has just returned home after a 2 week absence!
- You just heard the news that the war has been settled peacefully!
- Your idea for a new recipe has been chosen to be in *Better Homes and Gardens*!
- You just found out that the string of bad weather is ending and the sun will return!
- That illness you were worried about has just been healed!
- All your anxiety about the future has been cleared and will not return!

DAY 22 ASSIGNMENT

Look for situations today that can give you more practice in feeling the good news. The more you practice, the more will come. Energy follows thought!

EVERY CELL IN MY BODY VIBRATES WITH POSITIVE IMAGES.

Set the intention to have the *Visualization Butterfly* fly into your dreams tonight.

Awareness

Higher consciousness gives you greater spiritual awareness of your life's journey.

Day 23

Awareness

We can become so preoccupied with the mundane aspects of life that we completely miss the gifts that Spirit is waiting to bring us. It is simply a new way of looking deeper at the ordinary.

The glittering purple in this image holds the vibration of Spring, the time of great awakening on earth. Your vision is attuned to see new life poking through the hardened ground as you celebrate the revival of life. So too, do you experience this revival when you allow Spirit to guide your vision.

The brilliant blue background reminds you that as you become one with Spirit, you participate more fully in the flow of life. All of your senses are heightened and your capacity to appreciate and treasure your blessings is increased a hundred-fold. Let this butterfly lift the veil of unconsciousness and know that in each encounter along the way, there is an opportunity for love.

EXERCISES

Being aware that there is something greater then what the self can observe may be difficult for some to comprehend. To deepen your connection with the unseen force (sometimes called God, Source or Universe) you simply have to heighten your awareness.

In your world today, busyness is the norm. Rushing to and fro in daily life leaves little time to practice present moment appreciation. Focus may be more drawn to drama and negativity than relishing blessings.

Today is all about noticing and savoring that which feeds the soul.

I greeted the day feeling safe and refreshed because:

My body was nourished today because:

I felt loved today because:

I extended kindness today to _____ and it made me feel:

I was pleasantly surprised today when:

My day went very smoothly because:

I was so proud of myself today when:

When I needed help today, I asked _____ and because I received it:

DAY 23 ASSIGNMENT

Read the statements to the left and as you go through your day be aware that you will be filling in the blanks tonight.

I FOLLOW THE FLOW OF SPIRIT AND AWAKEN TO A WORLD OF BLESSINGS.

I will dream that I am aware of every single blessing that flows into my life!

Wisdom

Step aside from your emotions and embrace the knowledge that all is in Divine order.

Day 24
Wisdom

Oftentimes, when challenging situations arise, we ask ourselves why me, why now? This butterfly is sent so you can reconnect with your higher Source. Behind the scenes we are being directed and guided on our journey. There is great comfort in knowing that all is in order.

The lilac and rose colors used in this butterfly are reminiscent of sunrises and sunsets. Just as you observe the cycles each day with the rising and setting of the sun, so too can you depend on your Source for inspiration and wisdom.

Orange carries the energies of joy and happiness, both of which flourish when you surrender in trust. Giving up your need to control brings you into a state of knowing that all your desires are fulfilled.

The next time the emotions of fear and helplessness overcome you, find this butterfly and remember that a greater Wisdom is at work. Participate fully in the journey, and trust the ways of the wise.

Exercises

As a child, most of us listened to fairy tales or recited nursery rhymes.

See how many images of *wise* you can remember:

_____
_____
_____
_____
_____
_____

As you got a bit older, perhaps you participated in a religious study, most of which had many venerable wise figures. Let us see how many of those come to mind:

_____
_____
_____
_____
_____
_____

So who or what is your Source of wisdom today? How often do you connect with this Source? Do you listen to this Source or disconnect and go on your way? Reflect on these questions and write down some thoughts:

Day 24 Assignment

Today's assignment is to connect with your Source as often as you can. Connect to ask for guidance if you are feeling confused, angry, sad, or lost. Connect to express gratitude if you are feeling abundant, blessed, lucky, or joyful.

I AM CONFIDENT AND CALM THAT ALL MY DESIRES ARE BEING FULFILLED.

Before going to bed tonight, reflect on the *Wisdom Butterfly*. This image connects you to your Source. Drift to sleep repeating softly the affirmation above.

Embracing your spiritual connection clears your path for inner guidance and clarity.

Day 25
Spiritual

In times of chaos and confusion, you find yourself searching for guidance. This search may take you to friends, family, or professionals. This butterfly shows you that there is another way through Spirit.

Purple is the color that carries the highest spiritual vibration. This color serves as a bridge connecting you and Spirit. As humans we sometimes stray from our spiritual path. We may become misguided and confused.

The background of this butterfly image shows how many paths can be woven into the tapestry of life. They all lead back to Spirit.

Spreading your wings, just like this butterfly, gives you the ability to soar upward. You are guided on a continuous journey with Spirit. Embrace your soul and welcome Spirit into your life.

Exercises

In today's reflection, the color purple is mentioned as one that carries a high spiritual vibration. That is due to where it is placed on the color spectrum. On a rainbow, purple is the outside color, closest to the heavens. In the Chakra System, purple is assigned to the top of the head, again closest to the heavens. But something having a high spiritual vibration can be quite personal.

Over the course of your life you have probably had many talismans or symbols of good luck. And what else is good luck but a blessing from Spirit!

Think back over your life and recall some of the symbols that have had meaning for you. (Don't forget to include your first blankie/stuffed toy!)

Time Frames	Symbols
Preschool age	
Grade School age	
High School age	
College age	
Young Adult	
Present Day	

Perhaps you are feeling as though you need a new symbol of Spirit, or a new way to connect that better represents where you are in your stage of spiritual evolution.

So many have disconnected from the spiritual practices of their youth and have never found a new connection.

What is your spirit missing and how can you bridge the gap?

Day 25 Assignment

This is a good day to ask others how they connect with Spirit (or any name they have given to something greater than themselves.) Consider the different answers you are given and see if one of them might resonate with you. Once you put the intention out there, Spirit will answer.

I walk the path knowing that I have Spirit's guidance.

Ask the *Spiritual Butterfly* to build the bridge to Spirit for you tonight. Happy trails!

Connection with the Divine gives you the understanding that knowing dwells within.

DAY 26

Knowingness

In today's society, much emphasis has been placed on formal education. College tuitions have reached a staggering amount of money and families are stretched to the max. This butterfly comes to give you another way of becoming educated, connecting with Spirit.

The lacy, iris-colored wings of this butterfly brings you a connection with the Divine. From this connection flows the wisdom and insight that guide you on your journey. You have all the answers within.

The twilight blue and teal affirm the presence of the Divine and help you to find the words to align with this magnificent inspired energy.

The white surrounding the butterfly represents the light. You feel safe within this cocoon of the Divine's expression. Simply visualize yourself in the center and feel the light radiating all around. In this presence, you know instinctively that your life is blessed.

Exercises

There are days when you may feel as though the heaviness and darkness are omnipresent. You may feel as though you have no answers for anything. It is really challenging during those times to remember all the situations that have come before and all the times you were able to resolve the difficulties.

Recalling the many times that you KNEW with certainty a direction, the right word to say, or the outcome can serve to provide you with a reminder that you DO KNOW when it really matters.

Try your hand at this below:

I knew I was loved when:
_____

I knew I had inner strength when:
_____

I knew I was happy when:
_____

I knew that everything would be alright:
_____

I knew that I could depend on _____ when:
_____

I knew that I was grateful for my life when:
_____

I knew that I could resolve to:
_____

Day 26 Assignment

After reflecting on the answers, are you feeling confident that you do know? Today, think about a situation that has been causing you to be stuck in a place of indecision. Know that your answer will be arriving soon. Say the following affirmation:

The presence of Spirit within is my center for all that I am.

The *Knowingness Butterfly* will encircle your dreams tonight. When you awaken in the morning, you will KNOW!

Inspiration

Know that you are being guided to make decisions that will support your highest good.

Day 27

Inspiration

Many times when we are faced with a decision, it is helpful to draw on a source outside your rational mind. This butterfly helps you to connect with a Source of information that will surprise and delight you. Being open to receiving is the first step of the process.

The purple shading used in this butterfly is representative of a high spiritual vibration. Purple has been used throughout history to denote royalty and positions of power. This butterfly will serve to empower and enrich your decisions.

Bringing in the color of amber works in tandem with the purple to create inspiration that holds the essence of heaven and earth.

This balance is necessary for you to receive heavenly inspiration and translate it into everyday application. The color pink in this butterfly acts as the mediator of both realms and allows for heart-centered decisions which are expressed fully in love. In trusting that your inspiration is always from a place of love, you are able to move forward with self confidence and make decisions that are for everyone's highest good.

EXERCISES

Well, here you are on the last day of your journey to inspiration! All of the reflections, exercises and affirmations of the past 26 days have brought you to a place of readiness and acceptance.

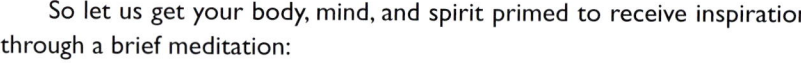

So let us get your body, mind, and spirit primed to receive inspiration through a brief meditation:

Take three deep breaths, and on the fourth one, visualize a purple light entering through the top of your head. Feel the pulsating and energy move from your head, to your neck, across your shoulders, down your arms, into your heart, down through the pelvic area and into each leg. Feel the warmth and heat radiating throughout your body.

Go within your sacred space and allow your inner soul to connect with Source. Visualize the purple light extending from the crown of your head to your Source. Know that you are now connected to infinite wisdom and inspiration. Choose a question that you have been struggling to find an answer to. Continue to breathe the purple light. Waiting. Inhaling. Exhaling softly.

Begin to notice a shift in your awareness, allowing you to receive an answer from Source.

What does it look like? What does it feel like? What does it sound like? You are inspired by the messages that you are receiving. Take a moment and feel how perfect the answer resonates within your soul. Know that this connection to Source is yours for the asking. The purple light will always guide you to this connection.

You can do this meditation whenever you are looking for inspiration.

DAY 27 ASSIGNMENT

You have now completed your transformation on seeing and connecting with the best parts of YOU. You have started and ended each day with a butterfly image. You have done the exercises and said the affirmations. Now your assignments are over, but a new journey is beginning.

The butterfly images and all their messages are now in your consciousness, ready to be recalled at just the right time. May they guide, enrich and empower you for healing and happiness.

I TRUST IN LIFE'S PROCESS TO GUIDE, ENRICH AND EMPOWER ME,

Sweet butterfly dreams all the rest of your days!

About the Authors and Artist

Ginny Zaboronek & Marge Richards
Butterfly Creators

The co-founders of Inspiring Butterflies bring a wealth of metaphysical training and experiences to their work. Both are highly schooled in the Chinese art of Feng Shui, the I Ching, the eastern philosophy of the Chakra System, Body Talk, Color Therapy, and Reiki to name a few. They have taught hundreds of students around the country in various methods of applying energy work. Integrating spiritual practice with a heart-centered philosophy based on unconditional love, their forte is in setting the stage so people can connect with their innate goodness and move forward in life with balance and joy.

Contact the authors at:

www.inspiringbutterflies.com
ginny@inspiringbutterflies.com & marge@inspiringbutterflies.com

Charlotte Garrett
Butterfly Artist

Charlotte Garrett was born in East Africa and started painting as a young girl. Her primary medium is watercolor. The subjects of her paintings include landscapes, nature close-ups, wildlife, coastal scenes, portraits, and pet portraits. She began showing her work publicly in 2003. Charlotte lives in Oriental, North Carolina. Find out more about Charlotte at www.garrettgallery.com.

Charles Garrett is recognized for his time and talent in graphically formatting Charlotte's butterfly paintings.

*May the Blessings
you have given to us
be returned to you
a hundredfold.*

~Ginny and Marge~

Notes

Notes

Notes

Notes

Notes

Notes

NOTES